Hot Cha-Cha!

Josephine Nobisso © Illustrated by Joan Holub

Gingerbread House
WINSLOW PRESS
Westhampton Beach, New York

To my daughter, Maria,
darlin' pooh-bar in the sidecar
J.N.

For Jay, Debbie, and Holland Gallagher
J.H.

In every conversation
'Bout the coolest situation,
The entire population
Wants the hottest information.

Tell us oo!
Tell us ah!
What's the brouhaha?
Tell us what happened with the cookie jar!

Start with **Who**
Start with ah
Start with hot-cha-cha!

Who found somethin' in the cookie jar?
Was it Hector?
Or Shanequa?
Or Ali' Kumar?

Harrison was hangin' 'round the cookie jar.

"You mean me?"
"Yes, you!"
"Couldn't be!"
"Then **who**?"

Maria put her hand in the cookie jar.

What

See a
See an ah
See an oo-la-la!

What did she find in the cookie jar?
Fireflies?
Or crackers?
Or the moolah-la?

Playground
is
Closed

Maria raised the key to the playground lock.

"The gate key?"
"That's **what**!"
"Glory be!"
"Jackpot!"

"It's here!" she told the kids up and down her block.

Playground is Closed

Playground is Closed

Why

Ask a
Ask an ah
Ask a doo-dah-dah!

Why'd she flaunt the key from the cookie jar?
To be fresh?
To be shockin'?
To be ha-ha-har?

So kids could swing so high that we'd almost fly!

"You say what?"
"We'd fly!"
"That's hot!"
"That's **why**!"

That key had been lost since the Fourth of July!

When

Check a **When**
Check an ah
Check an oom-pah-pah!

When did you pump the swings
and have some fun?

In the mornin'?
In the evenin'?
Or when work was done?

We flew at noon
toward a croonin' sun.

"At high noon?"
"That's **when**!"
"So soon?"
"Amen!"

The Tangle Team turned up
to double-dutch 'til one!

Where

Find a
Find an ah
Find a siss-boom-bah!

Where did you fly to on this great big Earth?
To Tunisia?
Or Korea?
Or to Amboy-Perth?

The banjo music swept us off to Fiddle-dee-dee!

"You went far!"
    "That's **where**!"
"Oo-fa!"
    "So rare!"

And Kimmi's gang all hula-hooped to Waikiki!

How

Know a
Know an ah
Know a la-di-da!

How'd Maria land to
    secure that key?
On a dime?
On a runway?
Or kerplunk at sea?

She traded her swing
    for a skatin' fling!

"Is that **how**?"
    "We'd vow!"
"Oh, wow!"
    "Know-how!"

And as we left the playground goin', "Skip and sing!"
The grown-ups crashed our party, tryin' everything:
The monkey bars, and seesaw, even leap-frogging!
We raced them to the sandpit, hoggin' every swing!
Then scoopin', swoopin', whoopin' we played tag-a-ling!

When I gave this education
To the nation's population,
   They sang, "Oo!"
   They sang, "Ah!"
   They sang, "Fa-la-la!"
Now we know your story⏤
The whole blah, blah:

Maria took you flyin'
toward the bright daystar.

Then the grown-ups took to slidin',
Yellin', "Hip-hurrah!"
Goin' gaga 'bout your wheelies,
Chantin', "Rah! Rah! Rah!"

HA HA HA HA HA HA

Callin', "Hoop-la!" to the jumpers
On the hot black tar.

Mom went freestyle on a runway!
What a superstar!

Laughin' ha-ha and a-hee-haw
'Til you collapsar.

Then Maria slipped the key
back in the cookie jar.

That's why we sing the praises of
the cookie jar!

The author wishes to thank:
Jane Snyder, Orel Protopopescu,
Suzanne Hulme, Elda Starke,
Pam Capozzola, Nancy Gannon,
Margie Nicotra, Brian Heinz, Karen Land,
EECBWI, Irene Gazza and Delta Kappa
Gamma, the Winslow crew,
the Riverhead and Westhampton Beach
schools, all the schools who've
had me in, the Golfos, Victor, Mommy,
Daddy al di là, and the Gospa.

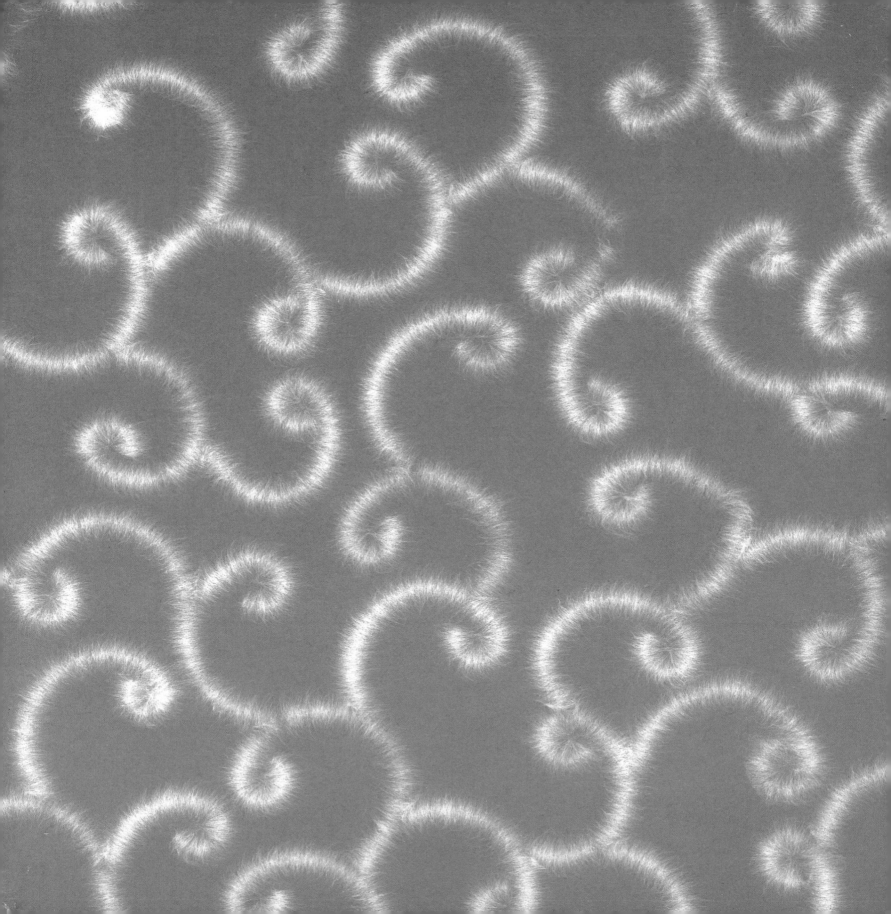